VALLEY
5069001
Gilbert  W9-BYS-917
The story of the Memphis
Grizzlies /

VALLEY COMMUNITY LIBRARY
739 RIVER STREET
PECKVILLE, PA 18452
(570) 489-1765
www.lclshome.org

THE STORY OF THE
MEMPHIS

GRIZZLIES

CREATIVE 🍎 EDUCATION

Published by Creative Education
123 South Broad Street
Mankato, Minnesota 56001
Creative Education is an imprint of The Creative Company.

DESIGN AND PRODUCTION BY **EVANSDAY DESIGN**

PHOTOGRAPHS BY Getty Images (Brian Bahr / Allsport, Lisa
Blumenfeld, Jonathan Daniel / Allsport, Barry Gossage / NBAE,
Elsa Hasch / Allsport, Andy Hayt / NBAE, Jed Jacobsohn, Joe
Murphy / NBAE, Panoramic Images, Gregory Shamus / NBAE)

Copyright © 2007 Creative Education.
International copyright reserved in all countries.
No part of this book may be reproduced in any form
without written permission from the publisher.
Printed in the United States of America

LIBRARY OF CONGRESS CATALOGING-IN-PUBLICATION DATA

Gilbert, Sara.
The story of the Memphis Grizzlies / by Sara Gilbert.
p. cm. — (The NBA—a history of hoops)
Includes index.
ISBN-13: 978-1-58341-412-5
1. Memphis Grizzlies (Basketball team)—History—
Juvenile literature. I. Title. II. Series.

GV885.52.M46G55 2006
796.323'64'0971133—dc222005051400

First edition

9 8 7 6 5 4 3 2 1

COVER PHOTO: *Shane Battier*

THE STORY OF THE
MEMPHIS
GRIZZLIES

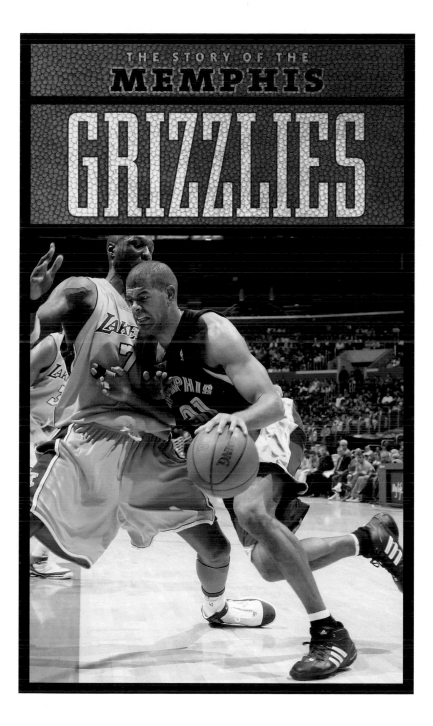

SARA GILBERT

VALLEY COMMUNITY LIBRARY
CREATIVE EDUCATION
739 RIVER STREET
PECKVILLE, PA 18452-2313

Almost every seat

IN THE HOUSE IS FILLED. MORE THAN 18,000 FANS
RISE TO THEIR FEET AS THE NEW MEMPHIS GRIZZLIES
CHARGE UP AND DOWN THE HARDWOOD AGAINST ONE
OF PROFESSIONAL BASKETBALL'S TOP TEAMS. *BEAT
L.A.!* THE CROWD CRIES. *BEAT L.A.!* IT IS NOVEMBER
10, 2004. THE GRIZZLIES ARE PLAYING FOR THEIR
FIRST WIN IN THEIR NEW HOME, THE STATE-OF-THE-ART
FEDEXFORUM. AND TONIGHT, BEHIND FORWARD PAU
GASOL'S 22 POINTS, THEY WILL SUCCEED AGAINST THE
MIGHTY LOS ANGELES LAKERS. AT THE FINAL BUZZER,
THE SCORE IS 110–87, A BLOWOUT THAT GRIZZLIES
FANS WILL LONG REMEMBER.

MEMPHIS GRIZZLIES
Memphis Tennessee

FOUNDING THE FRANCHISE

AROUND 3500 B.C., THE ANCIENT EGYPTIANS established their capital city along the banks of the Nile River and named it Memphis. More than 5,000 years later, in 1819, United States General and future president Andrew Jackson founded a new settlement along the banks of the Mississippi River in Tennessee and called it the same.

During its first 150 years, Memphis, Tennessee, became famous for its export of cotton and the development of blues music. In recent years, it has drawn millions of tourists eager to see Graceland, the home of legendary singer Elvis Presley. In the summer of 2001, a new attraction arrived in Memphis: a National Basketball Association (NBA) franchise called the Grizzlies.

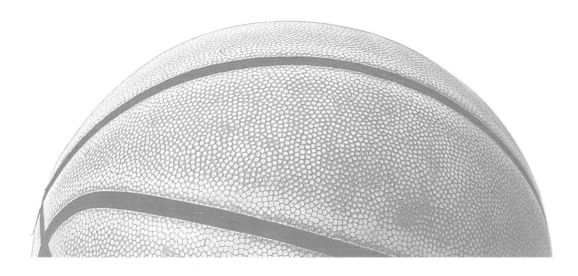

Greg Anthony, who would later go on to become a television analyst, was among the original Grizzlies

10

Despite his great size, center Bryant "Big Country" Reeves showed a surprisingly soft shooting touch

The Grizzlies started out nearly 2,000 miles north of Memphis in Vancouver, British Columbia, where local businessman Arthur Griffiths gained approval for the franchise from the NBA in February 1994. Griffiths chose Stu Jackson, a former NBA and college coach, as the Grizzlies' first president and general manager.

Jackson hired Atlanta Hawks assistant coach Brian Winters as the team's head coach. Together, Jackson and Winters selected 13 players in an NBA Expansion Draft, including point guard Greg Anthony, veteran shooting guard Byron Scott, and speedy swingman Theodore "Blue" Edwards. The club then looked to add a "man in the middle," a bruising center who could score, rebound, be a defensive force under the basket, and resonate with fans as well. The Grizzlies got all of those qualities in their first-ever NBA Draft pick, Bryant "Big Country" Reeves out of Oklahoma State University.

Reeves had a strong inside game and a willingness to learn that earned praise from coaches and scouts around the country. "I've always liked his game," commented Bill Walton, a former All-Star NBA center and television analyst. "He's learned the physical part of the game. All the raw material, all the potential, is there."

LONG LOSING STREAK

Few teams play their way into the NBA record books in their first season. But the Vancouver Grizzlies did it with a 23-game losing streak that set the mark for the most consecutive losses in a single season. Between February 16, 1996, and April 2, 1996, the Grizzlies lost every single game. It wasn't until they took on the Minnesota Timberwolves on April 3 that they were able to squeak out a 105–103 last-second win and snap the skid. "I think we'd forgotten what it feels like to win," veteran swingman Blue Edwards said after sinking the winning shot with eight-tenths of a second left in the game. The Grizzlies' dubious record is today shared with the Denver Nuggets, who lost 23 straight games during the 1997–98 season.

ABDUR-RAHIM TO THE RESCUE

ALTHOUGH REEVES AND THE GRIZZLIES WON THEIR first two games in 1995–96, reality soon set in. The Grizzlies lost their next 19 games before finally defeating the Portland Trail Blazers in overtime in their 22nd game. Injuries late in the season led to another downward spiral. This time, the club lost 23 games in a row, setting a dubious NBA record.

Still, Vancouver fans packed General Motors Place for nearly all of the team's home games and took pride in how hard their undermanned Grizzlies played. After the season, Stu Jackson set out to reward the fans' faith in the new team by improving it. His first step was to get some help for Reeves. Before the 1996 NBA Draft, the Grizzlies traded for forwards Pete Chilcutt and George Lynch. They also signed sharpshooting guard Anthony Peeler to provide instant offense from the outside.

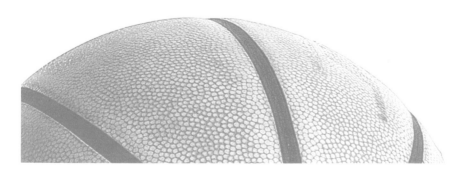

FORWARDS

Although he could slash to the rim, Anthony Peeler was best known for his long-range shooting

At a chiseled 6-foot-9 and 230 pounds, Shareef Abdur-Rahim was a phenomenal all-around athlete

Then, with the third overall pick in the NBA Draft, Vancouver selected 19-year-old forward Shareef Abdur-Rahim, who had decided to turn pro after only one season at the University of California. Abdur-Rahim had led the Cal Golden Bears in scoring, rebounding, and steals and had become the first freshman ever named Pac 10 Conference Player of the Year. In his first year in Vancouver, Abdur-Rahim averaged 18 points and almost 7 rebounds per game. He would improve on those numbers in his second and third seasons, ranking sixth and then fourth in the NBA in scoring.

"He's an extremely hard worker, particularly in the off-season, not only on his game but on his body," Jackson said of Abdur-Rahim. "He believes all the great players who have played in this league continually add to their games. After every season, he comes back a better player."

THE BIRTH OF A BEAR

When businessman Arthur Griffiths started the process of bringing a professional basketball team to Vancouver, British Columbia, he intended to call the new club the "Mounties," after the Royal Canadian Mounted Police, who wear striking red uniforms, stiff, wide-brimmed hats, and tall, leather boots as they ride handsome horses on patrol. But the real Mounties objected to the use of their name for the team, and Griffiths faced trademark problems as well. So, when Griffiths and Stu Jackson, the team's president and general manager, officially introduced the team to Vancouver on August 11, 1994, at the University of British Columbia's Museum of Anthropology, they went with their second choice: the Grizzlies, named for the strong, fierce bears indigenous to Canada's westernmost province.

THE WILDCAT CONNECTION

ALTHOUGH ABDUR-RAHIM AND THE GRIZZLIES WERE indeed getting better, the team still lost too many close contests. Fortunately, talented players continued to arrive in Vancouver. In the 1998 NBA Draft, the Grizzlies selected point guard Mike Bibby, who had led the University of Arizona Wildcats to the college national championship just months earlier. Bibby was a great ball handler who cared more about giving his teammates scoring opportunities than padding his own statistics.

During his second season with the Grizzlies, Bibby was joined by former Arizona teammate Michael Dickerson. Dickerson arrived via a blockbuster trade with the Houston Rockets for the Grizzlies' top pick in the 1999 NBA Draft, guard Steve Francis. The "Wildcat Connection"

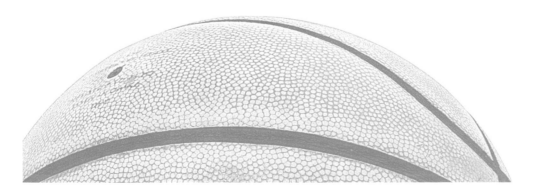

FORWARD

Even though he was barely six feet tall, Mike Bibby found his way past even the biggest opponents

17

18

Stromile Swift had a knack for blocking shots on defense and creating his own shots on offense

gave the Grizzlies one of the top young guard duos in the league. Together, Bibby and Dickerson averaged 32 points and nearly 11 assists per game in 1999–00 as the team finished a disappointing 22–60.

Three other key figures arrived in Vancouver in 2000. The Grizzlies traded for backup center Isaac Austin and selected forward Stromile Swift in the 2000 NBA Draft. New general manager Billy Knight (who replaced Jackson midway through the 1999–00 season) described the athletic, 6-foot-9 "Stro" as "a young colt ready to stand in the winner's circle."

The third key addition was head coach Sidney Lowe. From his college days as point guard on the 1983 "miracle" college champion North Carolina State Wolfpack team to his years in the NBA as a player and coach, Lowe had learned that the secrets to winning are defense and teamwork. Lowe made it clear that he expected hard work from his players and assured fans that the hard work would produce winning results.

But the club continued to struggle in 2000–01. As the team stumbled to a 23–59 finish, fan support dwindled. After the season, a major shakeup took place. In one amazing week, Abdur-Rahim was traded to the Atlanta Hawks for the draft rights to Spanish forward Pau Gasol; the club drafted Duke University forward Shane Battier, the College Player of the Year; and Mike Bibby was sent to the Sacramento Kings in exchange for one of the league's flashiest point guards, Jason Williams.

Jason Williams's flair for fancy dribbling and trick passing entertained Grizzlies fans for four seasons

GOOD HAIR DAY

When the Grizzlies drafted 7-foot and 292-pound Bryant "Big Country" Reeves with their first pick in the 1995 NBA Draft, fans in western Canada immediately fell for the large, lovable center. Bryant's down-home charm was so appealing that the Grizzlies sponsored a special "Hair Country" promotion on January 7, 1996. All fans willing to have their hair shaved in a flattop like Big Country's would receive two free tickets to that night's game. The team expected a couple hundred people to show up, but by game time, more than 10 times that number were in line to get buzzed. Reeves was blown away by the show of support. "When 2,000 people show up to get their hair cut," he said, "you know you've got a lot of fans."

MOVING TO MEMPHIS

THE GRIZZLIES HAD REVAMPED THEIR LINEUP, BUT the biggest change was still to come. Less than a week after the 2001 NBA Draft, the NBA's Board of Governors approved the sale of the Grizzlies to a group of businessmen in Memphis. So, the team said good-bye to the Pacific Northwest and moved from Canada to Tennessee.

The new Memphis Grizzlies opened the 2001–02 season with an eight-game losing streak. Although they would finish the season just 23–59, the play of Battier and Gasol, who earned NBA Rookie of the Year honors, offered hope to the team's new Southern fans. Lorenzen Wright, a former University of Memphis star, also impressed the hometown crowd with several big performances, including a 33-point game against the Dallas Mavericks in November.

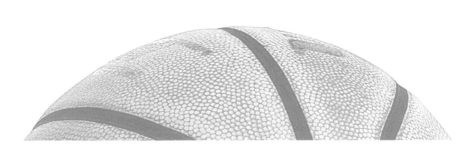

23

Seven-foot forward Pau Gasol averaged 17 points and almost 9 rebounds a game as an NBA rookie

24

Mike Miller and the Grizzlies showed improvement late in 2002–03, winning six games in a row

Before the 2002–03 season, the Grizzlies brought in Jerry West, a longtime player, coach, and executive for the Los Angeles Lakers, as team president. West said that he came out of retirement for the sole purpose of building a winning franchise. "This opportunity gives me a challenge to do something unique," West said. "I have always wondered how it would be to build a winning franchise that has not experienced much success."

The winning didn't come easily, however. The Grizzlies again started the season with eight straight losses, and coach Sidney Lowe was fired. Under new coach Hubie Brown, the Grizzlies lost another five games before rebounding to finish the season 28–54, their best record yet. Gasol netted 19 points per game to lead the team in scoring, Williams led the team in assists, and forward Mike Miller, a former Rookie of the Year with the Orlando Magic, added offensive spark. Although the team's eighth season ended with an eighth losing record, the Grizzlies seemed to be headed in the right direction.

WEST HEADS SOUTH

Jerry West had spent his entire basketball career with the Los Angeles Lakers—14 years as a player, 4 as a coach, and more than 20 in the front office—when the Memphis Grizzlies called in the spring of 2002. In April of that year, West became the new president of basketball operations for the Grizzlies—and found himself back home in the South "I was never really a West Coast guy," West said. "I grew up in West Virginia, and I'm familiar with the culture of this area. These are friendly, gracious, warm people. If anything, Los Angeles was the biggest culture shock for me when I went there." Although West now works behind the scenes, his on-the-court image remains prominent. His signature drive to the hoop is depicted in the player silhouette of the NBA logo.

PLAYOFF BOUND

THE GRIZZLIES WERE DETERMINED TO LET OUT A roar in 2003–04, and they did, thanks in part to the addition of forwards James Posey and Bo Outlaw and the continued improvement of guard Earl Watson. By the end of February 2004, Memphis had 30 wins, already a franchise record. The team won 13 of 15 games in March and ended the season 50–32, almost doubling their previous best win total. Hubie Brown was named NBA Coach of the Year as the Grizzlies made their first playoff appearance.

Versatile 6-foot-8 forward James Posey gave Memphis veteran leadership and tough defensive play

GRIZZLIES

Fans expected big things from Hakim Warrick, who was known as a high-flying scorer at Syracuse

Although the Grizzlies were swept in the first round by the powerful San Antonio Spurs, they were back for another run the next season. After health problems forced Coach Brown to retire early in the season, Mike Fratello stepped in and helped the 2004–05 Grizzlies amass 45 wins on their way to a second straight playoff appearance. The Grizzlies were again swept in the first round, this time by the Phoenix Suns, but their young lineup took a positive outlook. "You always learn from mistakes and losses," Gasol said after the loss. "It's hard right now. Maybe after watching and seeing yourself [in a replay of the game] you can learn, but right now it is just painful."

Hoping to improve their playoff fortunes, the Grizzlies continued to stockpile talent in the off season, adding Hakim Warrick, a 6-foot-9 forward from Syracuse University, through the 2005 NBA Draft. "He's long, he's an athlete, he gives us flexibility as far as where he'll play," said Coach Fratello. "He's a player. This is a quality young man that we drafted."

The Grizzlies franchise suffered serious growing pains during its early years in the NBA, but today, settled in a new home and featuring a new attitude, the team is eager to continue clawing its way up the standings in Tennessee. One of the youngest franchises in the league, the Memphis Grizzlies hope to grow by leaps and bounds in the seasons to come.

THE NEW DEN

On November 3, 2004, the Grizzlies started a new season in a new home: the FedExForum, a $250-million, state-of-the-art arena built for the team in the heart of Memphis's entertainment district. The arena, built with fine dining options, a sports bar, and the latest stadium technology, was packed to capacity, and all 18,119 fans wanted to see the Grizzlies crush the Washington Wizards. But the Grizzlies lost 103–91 that night and didn't win until November 10, when they topped the Los Angeles Lakers 110–87 at home. "We finally played the way we are capable of playing and closed out the ballgame," said Grizzlies forward Mike Miller. The FedExForum also houses the Rock 'n' Soul Museum and hosts concerts and family shows.

31

Scrappy point guard Earl Watson helped power the Grizzlies to the 2004 and 2005 playoffs

VALLEY COMMUNITY LIBRARY
739 RIVER STREET
PECKVILLE, PA 18452-2313